Why Did You Put That Needle There?

Why Did You Put That Needle There?

And other questions commonly heard inside an acupuncture clinic, with their answers.

Andy Wegman

Andy Wegman

Editing: Cris Monteiro, Tracy LaCreta, Jennifer
Woolf, Mary Cole

Cover Art: David Grant (www.bchiclitz.com)
Interior Artwork: Dave Rioux

Made in Manchester, NH

The information found in this e-book is also
available as free audio book at:

www.manchesteracupuncturestudio.org

Forward

Introduction

Common Questions and Their
Answers:
Sections 1, 2 and 3

Resources and Recommended
Reading

Thank You

Index of Questions

Forward

A man who will usually sleep soundly for 45 minutes during his acupuncture treatments was beckoning me over to his recliner only a short while after I had initially left him. "I've got an idea for a book you're going to write". AD whispered quickly, urging me to write down the title and general idea that came to him. "Write it like you say it to everyone", he directed. I immediately appreciated his idea, and loved the fact that it was inspired during a treatment. Some of my own best thinking has been done in the twilight of acupuncture treatments as well.

AD had recently come to discover and love acupuncture. In particular, he was fond of the community acupuncture clinic model that allowed him to afford regular treatments. He also made sure to mention how much he appreciated the transparency, sense of humor, frank talk and casual culture of the community clinics he'd visited.

After I nodded to affirm that I got it all down on paper, he closed his eyes and eased back alongside several others in a scene that would repeat itself day after day in our clinic and in an increasing numbers of community clinics around the country, over the following months.

~~~~

It is due to the hundreds of people we see each week in our clinic for whom acupuncture is something very new - and thousands experiencing it for the first time elsewhere - that I decided to follow through with this project. This while also knowing how useful information like this would've been for me as a newer practitioner in years past.

I have not come by such a direct and practical question and answer collection like my friend AD has proposed - and certainly not with an emphasis on the burgeoning community acupuncture social-business/justice movement.

I'm wanting this information to speak to new friends who may ask similar questions over the next few years ahead; the years before widespread access to affordable acupuncture allows millions to get themselves treatments as readily as we now can grab a slice of pizza and a cup of coffee in our neighborhoods. When a book like this may not be needed any longer.

Onward.

Andy Wegman
Manchester, NH
Spring 2010

Introduction

This is a book of questions most commonly asked of us in our acupuncture clinic and the best answers we have to offer. It's been compiled and written to ease worry for those who are new to acupuncture – on either side of the needle.

The participating writers of this project all work together at Manchester Acupuncture Studio - a community acupuncture center located in Manchester, NH USA. At the time of writing, the center is giving 350+ treatments each week. We mention this only to demonstrate our qualifications to recognize *commonly asked* questions.

Our collective experiences as acupuncturists tell us acupuncture is gracefully simple to use and the necessary tools are few and inexpensive. Because of this, we know it has the potential to play a significant role in reducing individual health care costs while increasing the well-being of our communities as a whole. This booklet aims to play a small role in this vision coming to pass.

Acupuncture is downright mysterious to most people we meet. Heck, it's often mysterious to many acupuncturists too. The fact that placing tiny needles on the arms and legs can lead to less suffering and improved mental and physical functioning is nothing short of wondrous.

Most importantly, acupuncture can also be profoundly

effective for a wide variety of common health problems, and so potentially quite helpful for many people. Really helpful. Helpful in unexpected ways. Helpful at times even when multiple medicines and surgeries haven't done the trick. And we know this only because thousands of people we've given treatments to have told us so, many times over.

We sincerely hope the following information takes some of the mystery out of acupuncture and makes it more inviting. Perhaps it will simply help to make a first treatment a bit more comfortable. It is after all, much better to take a sweet 'needle nap' without having questions running through one's mind.

~~~~

Note to the Reader: Feel free to take on these topics in the order written or drop into the conversation entry to entry as you see fit.

<u>Common Questions and Their</u>
<u>Answers</u>

Section 1) The Bigger
Picture

Section 2) While Getting
Treated

Section 3) Questions only
heard in a Community
Acupuncture clinic

1
The Bigger Picture

1) What is acupuncture?

Let's first define the terms:

The term 'acupuncture' comes from the Latin 'acus' (point) and 'punctura' (to prick)[1].

Here are the Chinese characters that refer to acupuncture: 'Zhen Jiu' signifying 'needle (and moxa) medicine'.

From Webster's online dictionary:

Main Entry: **acu·punc·ture**
Pronunciation: \-ˌpəŋ(k)-chər\
Function: *noun*
Date: 1684
An originally Chinese practice of inserting fine needles through the skin at specific points especially to cure disease or relieve pain.

This seems as good a quick definition as any.

We'll offer up another with a little more detail:

Acupuncture is one of the oldest, most common and dependable medical therapies used in the world. It is by nature simple, safe and effective health care.

---

1   George Soulie de Morant, Chinese Acupuncture, 1994, Paradigm
    Publications, Brookline, MA

Acupuncture practitioners use thin, sterile disposable needles inserted superficially into specific areas of the body in order to help the body's ability to heal itself.

Over the three decades or so in which acupuncture has gained popularity in the United States, it has been proven by an increasing body of scientific evidence to be not only exceptionally safe[2], but statistically effective as well.[3]

2) What am I supposed to feel during a treatment?

In general, it's safe to say receiving acupuncture should make you feel calm and sleepy once needles are placed. Commonly, people will feel either oddly heavy or quite light as they lay quietly in recliners or on tables for the duration of treatment time. Most fall asleep or doze quietly.

3) Why would I want to get acupuncture?

People get acupuncture for many different reasons. For our purposes, we'll offer two main answers to this question.

A) Here is a list of conditions the World Health Association has deemed appropriate for treatment with acupuncture.[4] They include but are not limited to:

---

2   http://www.nationalacupuncturefoundation.org/pages/publications/safety_chart.html
3   Examples include:
    http://www.umm.edu/news/releases/acupuncture.htm,
    http://www.sciencedaily.com/releases/2010/02/100204075105.htm,
4   Zhang X. *Acupuncture: Review and Analysis of Reports on Controlled Clinical Trials.* Geneva: World Health Organization, 2002. The World Health Organization

Adverse reactions to radiation and/or chemotherapy
Allergic rhinitis (including hay fever)
Biliary colic
Depression (including depressive neurosis and depression following stroke)
Dysentery, acute bacillary
Dysmenorrhoea, primary
Epigastralgia, acute (in peptic ulcer, acute and chronic gastritis, and gastrospasm)
Facial pain (including craniomandibular disorders)
Headache
Hypertension, essential
Hypotension, primary
Induction of labour
Knee pain
Leukopenia
Low back pain
Malposition of fetus, correction of
Morning sickness
Nausea and vomiting
Neck pain
Pain in dentistry (including dental pain and temporomandibular dysfunction)
Periarthritis of shoulder
Postoperative pain
Renal colic
Rheumatoid arthritis
Sciatica
Sprain
Stroke
'Tennis elbow'/Golfer's elbow - epicondylitis
Abdominal pain (in acute gastroenteritis or due to gastrointestinal spasm)
Acne vulgaris
Alcohol dependence and detoxification
Bell's palsy
Bronchial asthma
Cancer pain
Cardiac neurosis

Cholecystitis, chronic, with acute exacerbation
Cholelithiasis
Competition stress syndrome
Craniocerebral injury, closed
Diabetes mellitus, non-insulin-dependent
Earache
Epidemic haemorrhagic fever
Epistaxis, simple (without generalized or local disease)
Eye pain due to subconjunctival injection
Female infertility
Facial spasm
Female urethral syndrome
Fibromyalgia and fasciitis
Gouty arthritis
Hepatitis B virus carrier status
Herpes zoster (human (alpha) herpesvirus 3)
Hyperlipaemia
Hypo-ovarianism
Insomnia
Labour pain
Lactation, deficiency
Male sexual dysfunction, non-organic
Ménière disease
Neuralgia, post-herpetic
Neurodermatitis
Obesity
Opium, cocaine and heroin dependence
Osteoarthritis
Pain due to endoscopic examination
Polycystic ovary syndrome (Stein-Leventhal syndrome)
Postoperative convalescence
Premenstrual syndrome
Prostatitis, chronic
Pruritus
Radicular and pseudoradicular pain syndrome
Raynaud syndrome, primary
Recurrent lower urinary-tract infection
Reflex sympathetic dystrophy
Retention of urine, traumatic

Schizophrenia
Sjögren syndrome
Sore throat (including tonsillitis)
Spine pain, acute
Stiff neck
Temporomandibular joint dysfunction
Tobacco dependence
Tourette syndrome
Ulcerative colitis, chronic
Urolithiasis
Vascular dementia
Whooping cough (pertussis)

B) In addition, we'll offer up a list of 'no-brainer' conditions – that is, situations that should absolutely be treated with acupuncture without hesitation:

Athletic sprain/strain, acute back and/or neck strain, temporal mandibular disorder (TMJ), Bell's palsy, headaches (including migraines), palpitations, early stages of cold/flu, asthma, tendinitis, arthritis, insomnia (poor sleep), Raynaud's, anxiety, high levels of stress, addictions, irritable bowel syndrome, reflux, hemorrhoids, many gynecological issues (including PMS), herpes zoster (shingles) and pre-/post-surgery for accelerated healing.

4) Do I have to believe in this for it to work?

Absolutely not. You only have to believe enough to show up a few times in order to give yourself the chance to see positive changes.

5) Do acupuncturists have to hold to some religious beliefs that I don't know about?

No. Acupuncturists come from as many varied traditions

of faith as your local banker, car mechanic or hair dresser. Acupuncture is born of *philosophical* traditions, not religious. It is given and received many thousands of times every day by Christians, Buddhists, Jews, Hindus, Muslims and atheists among others.

6) So....how does all this work?

This is really the million-dollar question. The easiest answer we can offer, *in bio-medical terms*, is that no one has a definitive explanation. There have been many attempts to nail down The One Reason acupuncture works, but to our knowledge no one has got it - yet.

In all likelihood there isn't *one* factor, but that many reactions going on at once involving different systems - including the central nervous system – that allow acupuncture to have such wide, strong and lasting effects. This can be seen by people predictably being eased out of the "fight or flight" response (sympathetic) into the "rest and recuperate" state (parasympathetic) once needles are placed during a treatment.

If you have been told or have read that there is **one** factor to account for how acupuncture works, that explanation is probably not the whole picture.

The most commonly referenced studies on the topic of how acupuncture works have been directed and written by Dr. Bruce Pomerantz, an American physician. Through his ongoing studies, he and his colleagues have found that the body produces measurable amounts of endorphins (natural 'pain-killing' chemicals) when receiving acupuncture. For a time, this was thought to be the breakthrough understanding for the mechanism of acupuncture's effect.

In our opinion however, there are limits to this explanation. For instance, his initial landmark study involved some very aggressive acupuncture needling followed by electricity added to the needles. It was only under these circumstances that the measurable amount of endorphins were identified. This does little to explain how much more subtle needling (like the sort seen in most acupuncture clinics) would initiate changes and cause reduction in pain or improve function, for example.

Dr. Pomerantz seems to acknowledge that his research conducted to this point, offers partial explanations.[5]

7) How soon will I start to see changes?

This depends on what you are wanting to be addressed, how long it's been present and your general state of health. Typically, short-term (acute) problems will respond within just a few treatments, while longer-term (chronic) problems may take up to twelve or more treatments before consistent change occurs.

This is a question that should be addressed with your acupuncturist during your first or second visit.

8) Will I have to come get acupuncture forever to keep feeling good?

Likely not, but this also depends on the reason(s) you're getting treated in the first place.

For short-term issues, a handful of acupuncture treatments should do the job. For chronic or long-standing issues, a

---

5 http://www.medicalacupuncture.org/acu_info/interviews /pomeranzart.html

maintenance schedule of some sort would be in order to keep systems running smoothly and steadily after the initial period of relief and change.

For example, patient Melissa comes in for help with pain and swelling from a new ankle sprain less than 24 hours old. This type of injury responds best with acupuncture treatments two out of three days, which would probably be plenty to help Melissa's body sort out her injury completely.

On the other hand, David gets acupuncture treatments to work toward better management of long-term anxiety and insomnia that he's struggled with for five years. Chances are good he'll start to see clear changes in the pattern and intensity of his symptoms with steady treatments over four weeks or so. After this time, his acupuncturist will likely recommend regular but less frequent treatments for another stretch of time to help make sure the process of change continues moving forward. Once David finds himself in a place where he's consistently happy with his sleep and anxiety levels, we'll know it's time to dial back the frequency of his treatments even further. The aim here is to provide as few acupuncture treatments as possible while maintaining gains made.

9) Should I call my acupuncturist 'Doctor'?

No, not unless they introduces themselves as such. Otherwise you should assume your acupuncturist is not a medical doctor. The vast majority of practicing acupuncturists are 'licensed acupuncturists', like a licensed electrician or licensed truck driver or building inspector.

Though licensing requirements vary from state to state, most licensing boards require between 1000 - 2300 hours completed over 3-4 years of study in an accredited school of Chinese medicine, in addition to a passing grade on the national board examination. This exam is brokered by the National Certification Commission for Acupuncture and Oriental Medicine (NCCAOM). All licensed acupuncturists are also 'Clean Needle' certified.

10) If I don't fall asleep, is the treatment working?

Yes. Though many people do take a nap of some sort during treatments, it still *works* even if you haven't slept at all. Lasting positive changes can absolutely happen whether it turns out you've been asleep or awake – or somewhere in between.

11) I have arthritis. How does acupuncture change the way my bones are shaped?

Acupuncture won't change this. But our experience tells us acupuncture can slow the progress of the arthritic changes, while helping your body reduce the inflammation (-itis) and swelling that often leads to pain and lack of mobility. We would expect acupuncture to help change how arthritic areas *feel and function.*

A series of acupuncture treatments can make arthritic joints less achy, less swollen and less susceptible to changes in the environment, such as moving weather fronts or changes in air pressure. This can all lead to practical benefits that can mean less medication, more independence, more productivity and better quality of life. Consider what being able to use knitting needles or knives or keyboards without pain can mean to people. Or to open a jar-top or door handle...

This is in part why we'd like to see many more people get

the chance to find out what acupuncture can do for them. It is no exaggeration to say we've seen people with arthritis get their independence, livelihoods and hobbies back as a result of access to regular acupuncture treatments.

12) Can I continue to do (therapy/activity) while I receive acupuncture?

As a rule of thumb, acupuncture is extraordinarily forgiving, and so the answer to this question is usually, <u>yes</u>. But let's look at this a little more closely....

In our experience the (blank) part of this question is usually taking medication, taking part in physical therapy or swimming or massage therapy or chiropractic.

In these cases acupuncture doesn't need to be done by itself. In fact, the benefits of acupuncture treatments are often seen clearly through the experience of other therapies. Some common examples:

We've heard many patients tell us their chiropractors have commented how much easier they've adjusted and/or their adjustments hold longer when receiving acupuncture. The same goes for people making faster gains in physical therapy, or noticing a need for smaller amounts of medications (or no longer needing medications at all) prescribed by their doctors.

This can go both ways, of course – where a patient may be stalling in treatment progress with acupuncture alone and a chiropractic adjustment or a new medication may get things kick-started and moving forward again.

If on the other hand, the 'blank' in this question has more

to do with maintaining an activity that irritates the problem, well that's a different story. Here's an example:

Larry comes in looking for help with chronic foot pain that's been more intense over the last two months. He finds himself limping most days recently and has had to take medication to help deal with the pain. At his third visit, Larry also lets us know he's been continuing to run five miles each day while coming for acupuncture, and he is frustrated with his progress thus far. In this situation it would be a good idea for Larry to take a break from running for a time and give his foot a rest and time to heal.

Acupuncture has a way of helping the body help itself. Its effects are like eating a good wholesome meal or getting an excellent night's sleep - except all at the same time. A man at our clinic recently described it like 'quietly rebooting your own hard drive'.

Although treatments can be quite helpful, you'll have to work with them – just as they are working with your own abilities to sort out illness or injury.

13) I'm not feeling well today, should I still get treated?

Most likely yes, if you can make it into clinic. If you are vomiting or have a very high fever for example, that's probably not the best time to come in. But if you are just feeling 'not well' or are coming down with a cold, those are great reasons to come in and get treated, as acupuncture can reduce the duration of a cold or stop it from coming on any further. Acupuncture can often point your body in a direction to take care of symptoms like this pretty quickly.

14) I take blood thinners for my heart. Is that a concern?

No. It's neither a concern, nor should it stop someone from getting acupuncture. In fact the idea of getting acupuncture to increase circulation, to ease the tension in the soft tissues - including the blood vessels - is something that can be especially valuable for folks with cardiac and/or vascular difficulties. Letting your acupuncturist know you take a blood-thinner is a piece of information they'd appreciate knowing, and is often asked in a health history questionnaire reviewed on your first visit.

15) Will I bleed?

Most often, you should not expect to bleed where the needles are taken out. Occasionally we may see a drop of blood due to a tiny vessel unseen just under the skin surface. This bleeding is stopped quickly with light pressure and a cotton ball.

16) Can I take a needle home to show my family?

Taking needles out of the clinic is a no-no. However, we're happy to offer the next best thing - pictures of what our two favorite acupuncture needles look like:

17) Can I take this needle home and stick it in that point if I get a headache again?

As much as we like to help you take care of yourself, we can't allow you to do this.

Keep in mind, acupuncturists are biased towards their favorite tool, like an electrician might be partial to a circuit tester. We rely on needles to dependably stimulate acupuncture points, but there are other ways to get effects. If you're really interested in manipulating your points on your own without needles, we're all for it and would be happy to show you how to do this. Ask us.

18) Do you sterilize your needles?

When people ask this, I think there may be an assumption that we are re-using needles. This is not the case at all. For the last 15-20 years, acupuncturists have used one-time use, sterilized, disposable needles as the industry standard. So there is **no re-using of needles** even from one part of the body to another.

Sterile package opened, needle in, needle out and put into a bio-hazard box to dispose of responsibly and that's it.

19) Do the needles hurt?

Not really much at all. However, getting an acupuncture treatment isn't always *painless*. More than anything a treatment should be a deeply relaxing and sleepy slice of time for you.

Here's what we'd like our patients to know: You may feel a bit of a pinch when the needles are tapped in, but this should ease right away. If you continue to feel a pinching or a burning sensation at the needle site any longer than this, *let us know*. It means we haven't placed that needle real well. If on the other hand you are feeling a slight ache or heavy feeling near the needle, this is usually a good sign – a clue that the body is reacting in a productive way.

The bottom line is that as long as the feelings around the needled areas don't keep you from closing your eyes and napping for a little while, we say let them be.

20) My symptoms come and go as a rule of thumb. Now that I'm feeling better, how do I know it's the acupuncture that caused this and not a phase?

Only time will tell. Our suggestion is to keep an eye on the overall pattern of your symptoms. For instance, if Nora's insomnia affects her at least two nights every week, and it's been 3 weeks since her last bout, this is a positive change in the bigger cycle. Hearing this, we'd be inclined to encourage her to stick around and continue treatment for a while longer.

2
While Getting Treated

21) Will you use the same points every treatment?

Deciding on point combinations depends on different factors. These will usually include verbal feedback regarding how things have changed since the last visit and from subtle cues our bodies give – such as variations in the pulses at the wrists and neck.

At the end of the day point combinations are chosen in order to give each person the best chance to see the greatest amount of change in patterns of pain or illness.

22) What are you injecting through the needles to make this work?

Nothing. And we couldn't if we tried. Needles that acupuncturists use are a filiform type, which means they are solid, not hollow like the type of needles 'shots' are given through (hypodermic syringe).

In fact, a standard-sized hypodermic syringe can hold about a dozen average-sized acupuncture needles **inside** of it.

23) You remember it's my back that hurts...why are the needles only in my hands and feet?

There are many ways to practice acupuncture; different styles, various techniques, emphasis on certain theories, alongside varied cultural traditions.

We like to think of it this way: an acupuncture needle is an instrument, like a saxophone. A musician can play that sax in a variety of different ways; within the blues tradition, the many types of jazz, country music, rock music etc. All in the effort to make music that *moves people* - either emotionally or physically.

Acupuncture points are chosen to achieve similar ends – to get systems *moving* in ways they haven't been to that point. This in order for us to function and feel better.

So as some acupuncturists tap needles directly into an area that's painful or not working well, others find treatments work out better if the needles are placed far away from this area of the main complaint. Ultimately this is a matter of preference on the part of the acupuncturist. And while initially it may seem strange to be using points on the arms, legs, ears and head for backaches, eye trouble, a stiff neck or belly aches, these are time-tested strategies that are particularly effective.

We happen to like to play our instruments in this way. It works for us, and reliably gets things moving for our patients.

24) Why did you put that needle there?

Because it's where your system needs to be tuned-up so you feel and function better. We know this from our own experience and from the experience of the many people who have practiced acupuncture for a very long time before us.

Acupuncture treatments are to our bodies like a tune-up is to your car or bike. A series of acupuncture treatments is like a block of maintenance. By getting 'maintained' we can reduce the chances of breaking down.

Acupuncturists figure out which parts of our systems need to be adjusted by following signals our bodies offer.

These clues can tell us where one area is limping along while others work too hard as a result. This is why we may feel pulses at your wrists or neck or take a peek at your tongue before picking acupuncture points to needle; to get a sense of where the tune-up is best directed at that time.

Taking this transit analogy further down the road...think of an area of pain or illness as a traffic jam along a main highway (I-93 around here). Here there's simply too much congestion in one place, causing rising temperatures, tempers and bad air. Choosing acupuncture points away from this over-crowding - for example in the hands or feet for a headache - is an attempt to open up exits and secondary roads around it. This allows for the traffic – various signals, blood, body fluids – a place to filter off, and get moving.

25) Why do you do this differently than my last acupuncturist?

As you may understand by this point in reading along, there are many different ways to approach people with the main tools of the acupuncture trade – namely needles, cotton balls and alcohol.

In addition, acupuncturists may also employ different tools and techniques beyond needling, e.g., cupping, moxibustion, gua sha (a.k.a. the Graston technique), tui na (Chinese massage) and of course Chinese herbal medicine.

This can all lead to a practice of Chinese medicine that can look pretty different from one acupuncturist to the next, and also why two practitioners might choose different points – even while working within the same clinic.

The main strategy is always the same however, no matter what kind of acupuncture is being used: The acupuncturist's job is to help the body to *fill what is empty and drain what is too full.*

We'd suggest the key for each person being treated is to decide if their relationship to the acupuncture itself and the practitioner feels good, in order to make sure there's a compatibility between both parties and the process itself. Knowing you are made to feel safe and taken care of is the best way to gauge whether you are in the right place. This and of course, making headway in your goals for treatment.

26) Can I drive after I get treated?

Sure, that should be no problem. While people react to treatments in different ways – from feeling relaxed or mellow, to energized and peppy - there aren't any specific activity restrictions following a treatment, beyond what common sense dictates.

You may not want to leave your favorite acupuncture center and run around one hundred miles an hour right away, but driving shouldn't be a problem. Some prefer to sit with a cup of tea or sip of water for a few minutes after acupuncture treatment. Most mosey on out without concern.

27) My pain went away and then came back again. Is this normal?

Yes, it can be and especially so at the beginning of a course of treatment for illness or an injury that's been around for a long while. It's not always the case that pain will fade away smoothly. Instead it can move around to different locations or change its nature (sharp to dull, dull to stiff) and then return again as it was before treatment.

This is all fairly common and ultimately a good sign.

What we're all looking for to begin, is *a change in the pattern of pain or illness*. Even if the change only lasts for a short time initially, this is usually a great sign for more consistent and lasting relief to come. Remember a course of treatment is a cumulative process with the effects of each visit adding on to the last.

This is one of the reasons why we recommend a cluster of treatments close together to get started, so the potential for a roller-coaster ride plays out quickly. And you'll know when relief arrives consistently – it speaks for itself! In the meantime, we recommend celebrating the smaller victories along the way.

28) Why do I feel sleepy once the needles are in?

To be honest, we're not sure. There have been many attempts at explaining why this happens and why acupuncture works in general (see question # 6). Our sense is, the presence of the needles causes our central nervous system to move into a clear pattern of rest (*parasympathetic*), allowing for our quickest healing and recovery to take place. Not unlike when we sleep at night.

This may explain why acupuncture is so effective at helping people overcome the many troubles associated with high stress levels – a state we can find ourselves in which is characterized by our nervous systems staying in a "fight or flight mode' (*sympathetic*) for extended periods of time.

Remaining in this state for long periods of time can keep us from recovering in an ideal way, leading to nagging injuries, sleeplessness or illness.

We can tell you, helping people get into a sleepy state is one of the most predictable and best effects acupuncture has to offer.

29) Why do I feel some of the needles, but not all?

Some areas that are needled are more rich in nerve endings than others – hands and feet much more so than the upper legs, arms or the belly for instance. These areas are going to be more sensitive by nature.

Sensitivity can also be a function of how close to the *bulls-eye* the needle sits. 'Head on' can feel like a dull-ache or sense of heaviness. A needle that's a bit off the mark may not feel like too much at all.

Feeling or not feeling a needle can also be due to the individual style of the acupuncturist – some of us are more gentle than others – or tend to pick among effective points that are more sensitive by nature.

30) The pain in my (injured area) began to hurt during treatment quite a bit - and then subsided completely. Is this normal?

Yes, it can be. While our bodies react to the effects of the treatment, the targeted area may feel tingly, warm, light - or infrequently - just plain hurt for a short while. These sensations are the result of the movement of blood and body fluids and are all great signs. The body is reacting, things are changing.

We'll refer back to the traffic on a highway analogy once again: as the traffic congestion (inflammation/pain) starts to ease and budge, what follows can be movement of the traffic (blood/body fluids) that is slow to start (tingling or pain) but eventually gets moving smoothly down the highway as it should (return to normal functioning and/or pain relief).

31) Even though we're treating (blank), my (blank) feels better - does this have anything to do with the acupuncture?

It's common for people to notice things changing beyond a main complaint during a course of treatment. This is one of our favorite aspects of giving treatments, and a reliable source of pleasant surprises for people new to acupuncture.

An example: Gill's main complaints are daily headaches and upper back pain. These symptoms are what he and his acupuncturist are focused on treating. Funny enough however, one week into his treatment plan, Gill reports his bowels are moving more smoothly, and his wife told him he wasn't nearly as grumpy as he had been in previous weeks. In fact, he shares his wife said, "you're a better person when you get acupuncture".

A favorite teacher of ours likes to say, "a million things happen when a single needle is placed." On a cellular level we'd imagine this is true. In answering question #31, we are suggesting a good deal of things are happening behind the scenes during an acupuncture treatment that both the giver and receiver of acupuncture are unaware of.

Though the goal of treatment may be to help manage incontinence or menstrual cramps or a sore elbow, during a typical course of treatment, bodily functions *in general* will predictably work more smoothly. This often translates into 'side-effects' that aren't necessarily expected, but certainly welcome.

32) Can I move during treatment?

Our recommendation is to try not to do a whole lot of moving around during treatment. At the same time, you don't have to lie like a mummy either. If you do have to move an area of your body where needles are placed, as long as you are careful and purposeful while doing it you shouldn't have much trouble.

Keep in mind your acupuncturist may end up asking you to move a specific area of your body while needles are in. Normally this will be the injured or painful area that brought you in for treatment in the first place.

An example: Erik's left shoulder is being treated for a mild rotator cuff strain. Needles are likely to be tapped around his knees, ankles and hand, but not the painful shoulder itself. Once needles are placed, it's likely Erik will be asked to move his injured shoulder gently every so often during his treatment time – as if it's a pot of soup cooking on the stove-top, stirring it around just enough so it doesn't stick to the bottom of the pot.

By doing this, Erik is helping to move blood and body fluids in to and out of the injured area. This is vital for healing to take place.

33) How many needles are too many? Too little?

Ask different needlers and you're likely to get very different answers. The number of points chosen in a given treatment can be a reflection of personal style, differences in training, type of condition being treated, relative state of health of the person getting treated, etc.

There are many different roads into the center of town. It's each acupuncturists job to figure out the best one to travel with each patient.

We think it's a safe bet most acupuncturists aim for the fewer needles, the better. In our clinic the average is about a dozen per treatment.

34) It felt like the needle was still there even an hour or so after treatment. Is that normal?

On occasion this does happen. When a needle helps to 'turn on' an acupuncture point, the body's response doesn't always stop when the needle is removed. This can include a lingering sensation that 'something is still going on' in areas that had been needled for a little while for some.

5% of folks will report back after treatment that one or more areas had continued to feel 'achy' or have a 'hum' to it for an hour or so after their treatment ended. This is nothing to be worried about, but all the same feel free to mention how you felt to your acupuncturist the next time you are in for a visit.

35) I felt a twitching sensation near the problem area during my rest. What does that mean?

It means the body is responding to the suggestions the acupuncture needles are making.

In our experience, folks most commonly feel things like a twitching sensation, a sense of lightness, heat *or* coolness, a heaviness or aching at the target area. As long as these don't keep you from relaxing or dozing off during your treatment, then it's not something to be concerned about.

These sensations are all clues that things are *moving* along. And that's really what an acupuncture treatment is all about.

36) How far do you put the needles in?

In general, only a few millimeters. But a more in depth answer depends on a few different factors:

The part of the body being needled... An acupuncture needle that is placed in the thigh is going to be brought to a depth a bit farther than a needle placed in the finger or on the ear.

The style of acupuncture is being used... Needle depth can vary anywhere from just above the surface of the skin, to just below. But again, this will vary with different techniques, styles and practitioner preferences.

The current season... The old medical classics suggest that needling should aim deeper in the winter, and the opposite in the summer. As the tree sap runs deeper in the winter than in the summer, acupuncturists are encouraged to go after the body's resources a little bit more in the coldest season.

*The patient's general state of health...*For a person in decent health, needles can be placed at an average depth. For a person who is in a fragile state of health, needles may be best tapped in just enough to keep them from falling out.

*The reason for treatment...*As an example, problems involving the skin are needled more superficially as compared to problems involving the bones.

37) When you put the needle in there, I felt it in a different place. Why?

Good question. We don't have an answer for certain, but have witnessed this happening with a number of people. For example a needle is placed in the right hand and immediate feedback is, "Oh, I felt that down in my left ankle."

We think it's best to admire this is a first-hand peek at the wondrous nature of our body's immense communication system.

38) My last acupuncturist used electrodes and wires on the needles. Will you do that?

We don't use much electro-acupuncture (EA) in our clinic. EA is the practice of inserting acupuncture needles in acupuncture points, attaching electrodes to these needles and running a gentle current through the area.

We have used EA and know it can be effective, but feel there are often other ways of achieving the same ends, more comfortably.

39) My last acupuncturist used burning herbs on top of the needles. Will you do that?

Although we love moxa (a.k.a. 'mugwort'), we do not use much of it in our clinic (more about community acupuncture below).

We will give moxibustion (the safe practice of burning moxa at acupuncture points) for homework if we feel it would be a good tool to have added to someone's treatment plan.

40) That really zinged, what did you hit?

Occasionally there is a circumstance where we'll hit *something*. If *something* feels like a brief electric jolt, we know this is a bulls-eye at an acupuncture point. This can be a fairly strong feeling, but will calm right away and is generally a good sign.

If on the other hand, the sensation around the point feels more 'hot', burning or sharp, this is generally a sign that the needle is not "sitting" well. In this case let us know and we'll fix it up right away.

Keep in mind, no sensations should keep you from resting very comfortably, plenty warm, and drifting along in your tune-up. Don't ever sit in pain while getting treated. If something is keeping you from closing your eyes and relaxing for a while, let us know.

3
Questions only heard in a Community Acupuncture clinic

COMMUNITY
acupuncture
NETWORK

Community Acupuncture (CA) refers to a particular social-business model. Its goal is to create increased access to acupuncture by offering treatments in a group setting all while charging fees on a modest sliding-scale with no income verification. In this way many people can afford to discover acupuncture and get treated often enough to see great and timely results, and acupuncturists can make a living doing what we do best. It's a wonderfully simple win-win endeavor for all involved.

The CA model started in Portland, OR at Working Class Acupuncture, where founders Lupine Hudson, Skip Van Meter and Lisa Rohleder have also worked to teach this model to other acupuncturists (and non-needlers too) who want to improve access to safe, effective treatments.

Lisa's terrific books 'The Remedy' and 'Acupuncture Is Like Noodles' are must reads for those who are interested in learning the reasons for and the how-to's of all things community acupuncture. Both are available at Manchester Acupuncture Studio and at www.workingclassacupuncture.org

In addition, The Community Acupuncture Network (CAN) is an excellent online resource for finding information about CA – including an up-to-date listing of affordable community acupuncture clinics in the US, Canada and elsewhere.

41) What's the difference between a visit to a typical acupuncture practice vs. a community acupuncture practice?

To start, a typical acupuncture practice in the U.S. treats each person in their own private room. Community acupuncture practices offer treatment in a group setting. We all know the value of power in numbers. Would you prefer to eat in an empty restaurant, or one that is full of people and vibrant? How about an empty movie theater? Us too! A healthy group setting creates a dynamic that can be used for all of our benefit in an acupuncture clinic. Receiving treatment in a community setting has other practical benefits as well; it's easier for friends and family members to come in for treatment together and many patients find it a relief to not be isolated during their treatment.

In addition, for many community acupuncture clinics, patients decide how long their treatment will take, as the 'right' amount of time varies from person to person, visit to visit. This can take anywhere from twenty minutes to a couple of hours.

Lastly, community clinics employ a sliding-scale fee schedule without income disclosure to help make acupuncture available to larger part of the greater neighborhood.

42) Am I missing out on good acupuncture points while in community acupuncture?

You aren't missing out on anything. No matter what style of acupuncture you receive or with whom, there will be excellent and effective points used, and good points that are not chosen. No one kind of acupuncture is able to use all of the acupuncture points at once – and nor should they...that would be a heckuva lot of needles!

We think your best bet is to leave the point selections to your acupuncturist, while giving them feedback about how treatments are helping to change patterns of illness or injury for you.

43) How will we be able to talk in the treatment room with so many other people in there with us?

This not a problem at all. Brief conversations between acupuncturist and patient are done chair-side while whispering or speaking quietly to one another. The treatment rooms have a good amount of space and 'white noise' between the chairs, so brief conversations aren't overheard by others in the room.

44) Will it work better if I rest with the needles longer?

Not necessarily. The basic answer to this question is, don't stay longer than you feel comfortable. When it's time for you to get moving and you want your needles out, just let your acupuncturist know by giving them a wink or nod.

It's just that simple.

We can tell you from our experiences, the vast majority of patients will know when their treatment time is up, and will then tell us so. Not the other way around.

This may seem odd to start, but trust us when we say 'trust yourself' with this one.

There are very few occasions when we'll choose a time limit for treatment. For instance, someone fighting a nasty cold or a flu would likely do better with a shorter treatment, say 20 minutes as opposed to an hour or longer. But this is the exception to the rule.

45) How can you afford to charge so little?

Because we treat lots of people. What's most important to a community acupuncturist is simply to give many people the chance to receive treatments. Likewise, the business needs to see many people in order to make ends meet.

Plainly said, we want acupuncture to be readily available as a means to help take care of the health our neighbors and communities.

46) Do I have to take my clothes off for treatment?

Absolutely not. Occasionally, we may need to have access to areas just above the knee or up to the shoulder joint, in which case we'd ask you to wear shorts or a tee shirt.

But by and large all it takes to get ready for treatment is to roll up pant legs and shirt sleeves, as points on the lower arms and legs are the most commonly used in community clinics. No need to take any other clothes off.

47) Could you please explain to me how the sliding-scale works, because I don't really understand?

The sliding-scale is a tool to help each person decide how much to pay for their treatment. We want you to be able to afford to come in for treatment as often as needed. The fee structure is here to help you figure out a way to make this financially possible.

The sliding-scales in community clinics are very simple in their purpose – you pay what you want, somewhere between $15 and $40 each time you come in, and that's really all there is to it. You decide what you pay, no questions asked.

We'd also like to make it clear regardless of what each person pays on the scale, everybody gets the same time and attention.

48) How long should I stay? How long do I have to stay?

We normally recommend to spend at least 20-30 minutes in a recliner with needles in. Anything beyond this is gravy. You are certainly welcome to stay as long as you want to. On average we'd say people spend about an hour in treatment, but the amount of treatment time is open-ended; there are no hard and fast rules.

Whenever you feel like you're 'cooked' or otherwise ready to get moving, let your acupuncturist know. In most community clinics, this is done by giving us a "purposeful look," such as a nod or wink or engaging our eyes. This way we'll know you need us and will come by right away. We trust that you know when your time is up, and we've learned by giving thousands of treatments that deciding treatment length works best this way.

49) What happens if I snore?

We're probably not going to notice and chances are you'll be in good company, regardless. Usually there is more than one person lightly snoring in clinic. If this is bothersome to other folks getting treated, ear plugs are available or they're encouraged to bring their favorite music player and pair of headphones.

To community acupuncturists, snoring is music to our ears on a number of levels: we know the snorer is very relaxed, and able to let it all hang out. Also, it's all part of the atmosphere of the clinic – the treatment rooms are safe places where people come to do a 'whole lot of nothing'. This includes taking a nice nap.

50) If I only have a half-hour to rest, should I still get treated?

We'd say 'yes'. A half-hour is plenty of time for a treatment to do its thing.

51) I've got a cough and cold and don't want to get everyone else sick in the treatment room. What should I do?

You should come in for treatment, no question. First of all, your acupuncturist will likely be able to keep your cough at bay during treatment so you won't agitate other folks in the room.

Second, acupuncture is an excellent ally during this time when our bodies are fighting off a cold, helping to rally resources to defend the 'castle'. Acupuncture will reliably help cut down on the length and intensity of a cold or flu.

Trust that your community clinic will be able to lend a hand when you need it, while also taking steps to keep other people in the treatment room free from catching your cold.

Resources and Recommended Reading

The Community Acupuncture Network
www.communityacupuncturenetwork.org/clinics

Lisa Rohleder, et al., Acupuncture Is Like Noodles: The Little Red (Cook)Book Of Working Class Acupuncture, Copyright 2009, Working Class Acupuncture, Portland, OR

Muhammad Yunus, Creating A World Without Poverty: Social Business And The Future Of Capitalism, Copyright 2007, Public Affairs, New York, NY

Michael Fine, MD and James W. Peters, The Nature Of Health: How America Lost And Can Regain, A Basic Human Value. Copyright 2007, Radcliffe Publishing Ltd., Oxon UK

Ted Kaptchuk, The Web That Has No Weaver, 2nd edition, Copyright 2000, McGraw-Hill, Columbus, OH

Lao Tzu, Tao Te Ching
(many different translations available)

The National Acupuncture Detoxification Association
www.acudetox.com

A Big Thanks To...

Friends and patients at MAS, Priscilla, Jeanne, Nancy, Carla, Judy, Sr. Agnes, Barbara, Shirley, Norma, Evelyn, Dr. Hsu, Lisa, Lupine, Skip, Korben, the CAN board past and present, AD, Karameeya and the Wegmans.

This book is dedicated to Ms. Elaine Lipson.

Index of Questions

1) The Bigger Picture

1) What is acupuncture?
2) What am I supposed to feel during a treatment?
3) Why would I want to get acupuncture?
4) Do I have to believe in this for it to work?
5) Do acupuncturists have to hold to some religious beliefs that I don't know about?
6) So....how does all this work?
7) How soon will I start to see changes?
8) Will I have to come get acupuncture forever to keep feeling good?
9) Should I call my acupuncturist 'Doctor'?
10) If I don't fall asleep, is the treatment working?
11) I have arthritis. How does acupuncture change the way my bones are shaped?
12) Can I continue to do (therapy/activity) while I receive acupuncture?
13) I'm not feeling well today, should I still get treated?
14) I take blood thinners for my heart. Is that a concern?
15) Will I bleed?
16) Can I take a needle home to show my family?
17) Can I take this needle home and stick it in that point if I get a headache again?
18) Do you sterilize your needles?
19) Do the needles hurt?
20) My symptoms come and go as a rule of thumb. Now that I'm feeling better, how do I know it's the acupuncture that caused this and not a phase?

2) While Getting Treated

21) Will you use the same points every treatment?
22) What are you injecting through the needles to make this work?
23) You remember it's my back that hurts...why are the needles only in my hands and feet?
24) Why do you put that needle there?
25) Why do you do this differently than my last acupuncturist?
26) Can I drive after I get treated?
27) My pain went away and then came back again. Is this normal?
28) Why do I feel sleepy once the needles are in?
29) Why do I feel some of the needles, but not all?
30) The pain in my (injured area) began to hurt during treatment quite a bit - and then subsided completely. Is this normal?
31) Even though we're treating (blank), my (blank) feels better - does this have anything to do with the acupuncture?
32) Can I move during treatment?
33) How many needles are too many? Too little?
34) It felt like the needle was still there even an hour or so after treatment. Is that normal?
35) I felt a twitching sensation near the problem area during my rest. What does that mean?
36) How far do you put the needles in?
37) When you put the needle in there, I felt it in a different place. Why?
38) My last acupuncturist used electrodes and wires on the needles. Will you do that?

39) My last acupuncturist used burning herbs on top of the needles. Will you do that?
40) That really zinged, what did you hit?

3) Questions only heard inside a community acupuncture clinic

41) What's the difference between a visit to a typical acupuncture practice vs. a community acupuncture practice?
42) Am I missing out on good acupuncture points while in community acupuncture?
43) How will we be able to talk in the treatment room with so many other people in there with us?
44) Will it work better if I rest with the needles longer?
45) How can you afford to charge so little?
46) Do I have to take my clothes off for treatment?
47) Could you please explain to me how the sliding scale works, because I don't really understand?
48) How long should I stay?/How long do I have to stay?
49) What happens if I snore?
50) If I only have a half-hour to rest, should I still get treated?
51) I've got a cough and cold and don't want to get everyone else sick in the treatment room. What should I do?